MOVING TO FLORIDA

Jo Thompson

AUTHOR: JO THOMPSON
ILLUSTRATOR: DAN TRAYNOR/MICHELLE MESSIER
COPYRIGHTS : JO THOMPSON

ISBN-13: 978-1978455399
ISBN-10: 1978455399
First Edition: 1981
Second Edition: 2017

TABLE OF CONTENTS

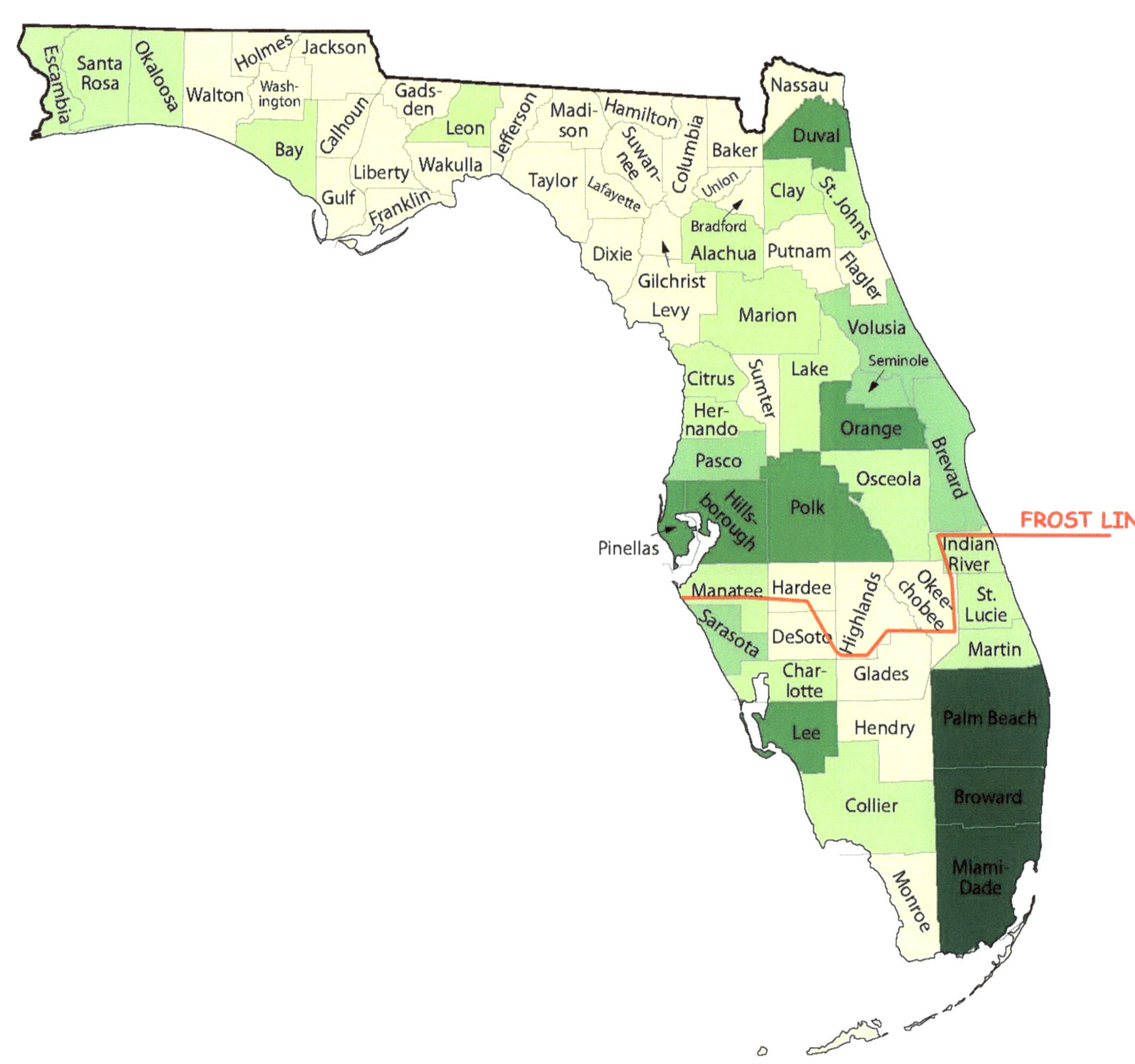

Escambia
Santa Rosa
Okaloosa
Walton
Holmes
Washington
Jackson
Bay
Calhoun
Gadsden
Leon
Liberty
Gulf
Franklin
Wakulla
Jefferson
Madison
Hamilton
Taylor
Lafayette
Suwannee
Columbia
Nassau
Baker
Union
Bradford
Duval
Clay
St. Johns
Dixie
Alachua
Gilchrist
Putnam
Flagler
Levy
Marion
Volusia
Citrus
Sumter
Lake
Seminole
Hernando
Orange
Brevard
Pasco
Osceola
Pinellas
Hillsborough
Polk
FROST LINE
Indian River
Manatee
Hardee
Highlands
Okeechobee
St. Lucie
Sarasota
DeSoto
Glades
Martin
Charlotte
Hendry
Palm Beach
Lee
Collier
Broward
Monroe
Miami-Dade

FOREWORD

So! you want a condominium, or a single family house, perhaps you may be thinking of a mobile home or even a boat to live on. What do you know about some of the rules and regulations? The purpose of this handbook is to acquaint you with some general information on all of the above plus other areas of general interest such as taxes, schools and some Florida trivia. You will even find suggestions on furnishing your new home and how to make mango wine.

This information is to give you a guideline on what to expect when relocating in Florida areas.

I hope you enjoy it.

WELCOME TO FLORIDA ~ THE SUNSHINE STATE

CHAPTER 1

WHERE? CHOOSING A LOCATION

On the enclosed map of Florida, I have drawn a line from Vero Beach to Fort Myers to divide the state.

This division is called the frost line. Below this line is the area that used to be considered by many people to be the best in Florida. Today, rapid growth in Central Florida has become, for many, the destination of choice. With the Disney entertainment area in Orlando, NASA on the Atlantic Coast, Pensacola Navy base in the Pan handle, Patrick air force base on the Atlantic Coast above Cocoa Beach.

After you locate the area of your choice, check it out in your computer by GOOGLING a county or city by name. It will give you a wealth of information on the surrounding area and its main attractions.

Your next step is to decide what your needs are. Are you looking for a retirement home, an investment, a vacation home? A retirement in the future? Or perhaps you are ready for a permanent move now. Your individual need may influence your choice of location.

ON YOUR OWN - OR WITH AN AGENT

If you have been vacationing in Florida for several years and choose that particular area for your new home, chances are you have become acquainted with its surroundings and have friends to help you locate just what you want and where you want it. You will also be familiar with the going prices of the local market and the facilities offered.

BUT - if you are not familiar with, or are brand new to Florida area, I recommend a real estate agent. You will save yourself time, gas, and headaches. Your agent will know the area thoroughly~ will be able to guide you and will help you determine what is best for your interests.

The agents will probably be your first contact and they will be most helpful. I recommend that you visit several offices until you find an agent with whom you are comfortable. Once you do, stay with him or her, and don't hesitate to tell him/her that you have been to other offices, and to say which properties, if any, you have been shown already. Aside from appreciating your candor, the agent will be able to save much time by eliminating duplication of properties shown.

Real Estate offices "cooperate" with each other, and generally each knows what the other has for sale. If you can't find what you want in the listings of that office, they will know about the listings of other offices and can arrange appointments to see the property. When you've reached a decision, they can present your offer and help you with the financial arrangements as easily as if it was their own listing.

Once you have stated your needs to the agents, give them time to research the area based on the information you have provided. You should be honest and not afraid to let yourself be QUALIFIED by stating what you need and what you can afford. This will make it easier on the agents to know what to show you. Why waste a day or more looking at $300,000 plus homes when all you can afford if $150,000.

Keep in mind that the coastal areas of Florida are considered "resort areas" regardless of the size of the town, the recreational or shopping facilities offered. Many properties are on or near the water, and a premium price is asked. Several miles inland can make a world of difference in price and what is included in it.

In addition to waterfront, golfing communities and some upscale retirement communities are also high priced. The golf course has become a fashionable setting. Today, there are 34,011 golf courses world wide with 45% right here in the United State at 15,372. The perimeter of the golf course has become the site for luxurious residential developments. The same house on a golf course, built two miles from the golf course, might be $100,000 more or less difference in price.

By-the-way, should you lose your deposit on a purchase for a primary residence, the Internal Revenue Service will not accept it as a loss deduction. However, if you are purchasing real estate as an investment, and you lose your deposit, it may be claimed as a business loss, be sure to consult your IRS office for further details and procedures.

HINTS TO SELL YOUR HOME

Florida is also a great place for investing in Real Estate of course. The sun belt is the fastest growing area in the United States. Although you may not consider retiring and/or living in Florida, a good investment now could provide the funds needed when and wherever you decide to retire. These investments may also provide the tax shelter you might need through your high earning years, which brings to mind that perhaps you may have to sell your present home in order to make your purchase in Florida. The following are hints to help you sell your home.

Before discussing the prospective sale of your home with a professional real estate sales person, make the house and grounds ready to pass a white glove inspection. A sincere buyer will be impressed by the cleanliness of the property and assume that the inner workings are in good order too. Remove all unnecessary clutter and furniture so rooms will seem more spacious. Increase the lightbulb sizes to the maximum for a warm cheerful look when the house is shown. Take care of the obvious maintenance jobs such as washing the windows, removing stains from the rugs, and cleaning out the kitchen.

If the lawn is well-edged and the walks are swept, the prospective buyer's first impression will be favorable and a freshly painted front door will generate enthusiasm. Pay particular attention to the appearance of the bathrooms, the kitchen and the children's play areas as they are usually priorities on the buyer's list.

Now comes the time when most errors are made. Trying to handle the sale yourself is a terrible temptation. If you set the price too high, no one will look at the house because it is not affordable. Too low, and prospects will want to know what is the matter with the property. Other than arriving at an asking price that will be in line with loan appraisals, just what can a real estate agent do that you can't - An experienced agent will draw from a background of previous sales in your neighborhood to help you set a price. He can also help you decide what fixing-up expenditures might be returned twofold. He wants to sell at the highest figure practical if his return is a percentage of the price.

He **will** direct advertising and listing campaigns, and hold "open house" as well as take care of "for sale" signs. He will answer calls day and night about assuming mortgages, house facts, neighborhood assets, schools and transportation, building quality and energy saving qualities. He will preview prospective buyers financially and give them guidance in obtaining mortgage money. He will represent you in promotions with multiple listers having interested buyers, and protect your interest during showings, offers and contracts. After closing he will make sure you are properly paid and provided with figures for income tax purposes.

As you can see, a real estate agent will save you lots of time to take care of other things which are always present in a major move.

CHAPTER 2

CONDOMINIUM LIVING

WILL IT FIT YOUR LIFESTYLE~
Economists predict that within 20 years half of the country will be living in condominiums.

Florida is increasing its share of condominiums faster than any other state. The latest census showed that there were 944,590 condominiums in Florida, and the growth continues daily.

Will it fit your lifestyle? If you are a young family, keep in mind that many condo's are adult communities, which means that children under a certain age are not accepted as permanent residents.

You must decide if this kind of close knit community suits your personality and lifestyle. Direct and personal contact with neighbors is more prevalent in condos than individual homes since properties are directly touching. Of course, the major asset to condo living is the relief from performing the maintenance associated with a home (mowing and painting for example). In condominium living, it is easy to meet new people, feel less isolated, form friendships and make acquaintances with people having similar recreational or social interests. Today Condos offer a wide variety of amenities such as indoor or outdoor pools, fitness rooms, entertainment areas, covered or outdoor parking.

There are many types of community living arrangements all headed under the condominium concept. They range from the medium to large high-rise apartments, to the townhouse concept, to the detached single family home in a condominium set-up.

Keep in mind that condominiums may have strict rules and regulations, most of which are geared to protect your investment, your privacy and your peace of mind. These rules are based on common sense, courtesy and mutual respect.

Though differing from project to project, the following generalizations apply to most condominiums. You, the owner, have title to the inner space only; your ownership usually stops just past the wall surface. The walls and what is inside them are common elements, as is the building exterior. You, as the owner, are responsible for maintenance inside the condo unit, the Condominium Association is responsible for the maintenance of the common elements; all those used by, or necessary to all residents. These common elements are where some of the monthly maintenance fees are spent. Recreational facilities and other common elements are for use by all owners, since all own an undivided interest in them (except in leased facilities.)

As owner of the unit, you will hold the deed to that particular unit you purchased and you will also own an undivided interest in the common elements of the community, such as hallways, elevators, pavements, and yards. All of the common elements will be well defined in the Declaration of the Condominium which is a compilation of the Articles of Incorporation and the rules governing the operation of the condominium community.

If you have young children or will have young children visiting you, they will have to be supervised at all times while on common grounds. They cannot be turned loose in the recreational areas or the clubhouse. Rules also apply to pets, and many places do not allow them at all; also some do not allow vans, trucks or motorcycles on the premises.

Condominium sale are regulated by strict laws enforced by the state of Florida. When you find the Condominium Community you really like, do not hesitate to put a deposit on a unit you choose.

You are protected by the "15 days right of recision regulation." This regulation allows the prospective buyer 15 days from the signing of the contract to study the condominium documents and consult with his attorney. (Look for this clause to be included on the contract you sign.) It is also a time for the buyer to consider his purchase.

Should you decide that you cannot accept these items, you've lost nothing as long as you notify the sales department WITHIN THIS 15 DAY PERIOD that you wish to cancel. Naturally, the sales staff may want to know the reason for your cancellation. Be honest and tell them; they'll appreciate your candor.

When you put a deposit on a new unit, a contract will be drawn up and all financial disclosures made to you at that time. You will choose your color schemes or whatever upgrade options you choose at this time also. Don't let it scare you.

It will save you time if you have to go back home next week and might even save you a trip back to Florida to choose all these if you decided that this condo is for you.

The following is what should be part of your Condominium Documents:

- Declaration of condominium
- Legal description, plot plan and survey schedule of percentage of ownership of common
  elements and common surplus.
- Article of Incorporation
- By-laws
- Estimated operating Budget

It is a good idea to have someone knowledgeable go over these documents with you during those 15 days.

Another method of acquiring a condominium is through resale. Many times the developer will have *resales* and your broker will know of some that are available. Check the newspapers yourself for direct contact with an owner. Really good buys can be found in this way since the owner may grant a purchase money mortgage to the prospective buyer. This mortgage means that the owner will lend you a portion of the selling price, often at a lower interest rate than those offered by the commercial banks. Price negotiating can also be discussed.

In the case of a developer, negotiating on price is seldom if ever allowed. However, when purchasing a resale unit in a condominium, you must be aware of the fact that the 15 days right of recision regulation does not apply. Also, with a new unit through the developer, you usually have a warranty that applies toward workmanship and appliances furnished, whereas on a resale unit this warranty is usually exhausted. In resales, as well as developer sales, it is also important to check on the rules and regulations that are in force at that particular community, because communities differ with respect to reselling a residence.

A few developments governed by land/recreation leases are still offered for sale, though the number of these are dwindling. A land lease means you have ownership of the building only. The owner leases the land to you and the "rent" will be reflected in the monthly maintenance fee which very often increases as the years go by.

A recreation lease is basically the same but, it is the recreation facilities that are leased to the owners. Here again the residents do not own this property and have no control of the costs with which they can be assessed.

It is also important to find out if the condominium community is managed by an outside management firm or if it is managed by the Association itself. Outside management can sometimes create problems which you will be unable to resolve. Experience shows that management through the Owner's Association is a more viable way of managing the community.

THINGS TO REMEMBER WHEN BUYING
A RETIREMENT CONDOMINIUM

Be careful of the location! It may have been fun to spend those few weeks on the beach away from the downtown during those vacations, but once the novelty of the pounding surf and the walks on the beach wear off, you begin to notice that the salt spray leaves a film on your windows that has to be cleaned off not less than once a week (a real chore.)

All the metal parts on your new apartment become pitted. Unless you have enclosed parking for your car, expect salt damage to it, which means buying a new car more often. The "no-see-em" population, a pesky gnat, is more prolific on the beach too and you may have to have your screens sprayed to deter the little bugger. Remember too that many of the beachfront condos are built on what are called barrier islands. Causeways are sometimes the only way to the mainland for your shopping, doctor's appointment, hair dresser, grocery shopping, etc.

In the winter months you can expect these to be crowded, and if the bridge is the kind that must be raised to let a boat go by, you might be delayed in traffic for awhile. During hurricane season, if a hurricane threatens the coastal area you are in, you may have to evacuate in a hurry. All these little things are not important, or just plain invisible, on a two week vacation, but when you have to put up with them on a permanent basis, you may want to think twice.

Riverfront (or canal) condos usually have less of these problems and are more apt to be near shopping centers. The salt spray nuisance is removed. In a hurricane, chances are that you will have to secure just a few items and not be asked to evacuate. If you are a boater, you have more chances of having docking facilities by or as near by your condo as feasible. Beachfront units very seldom provide docking facilities. Recreation facilities such as bowling alleys, craft shops, and shopping areas will be more varied and be more abundant in off-beach condominium communities.

If you have doubts that condo living is for you, rent one for six months to a year before making your decision.

IF ALL YOU WANT IS
A VACATION HOME

If you are still working full time and raising a family and only have one or two weeks a year to enjoy your vacation, Interval Ownership (also called Time-Sharing) may be for you. There are two basic kinds of interval ownerships. The first is deeded, fee simple ownership. This is the most popular form in Florida because it provides good security for its buyers since, when you make a purchase, you buy into a condominium just as you would any real estate. The only difference is that your deed specifies a particular time each year that you may use the property. The deed may be willed to your heirs, resold, and you can deduct your ad valorem taxes on the property from your income taxes.

The second type of interval ownership is Right-to-Use, non-ownership. With this you will receive a license to occupy a unit for a specified period of time each year. "Right-to-use" contracts can range from 10 to 40 years, but since the developer retains the title to the property you often have limited rights and privileges.

In both of the above, one week is set aside for annual maintenance. Each one week period represents 1/51 percent ownership in the building and land. The average purchase is 2.6 weeks, and the apartment is jointly owned by about 19 other families. Because one shares in the ownership of the apartment, one must also share in its upkeep costs. Prices of course will vary substantially and are based. on location of the resort, size of the unit, and the time of the year you select for your use. An average purchase price for each week is approximately $19,000 with and approximate annual maintenance fee of $660.00. Don't forget that this, as in all real estate transactions depend on location, location and location.

This fee is used for maintaining the grounds and recreational facilities such as the pool, tennis courts and any other amenities that exist. Some of the money is also set aside to replace furniture, carpeting and fixtures as they wear out. Under Florida's guidelines, no management company is allowed to raise these maintenance fees more than 15 percent per year. If this is the type of vacation home that will suit you, an added feature to look for is the type that offers interchangeable ownership; which means you may spend your vacation in another area if the time is available when you want it.

It is not necessary for someone to take your condominium for an exchange to take place. All that is necessary is for a condominium to be free at the desired location. As long as your condominium is put into the exchange system, it is not necessary for you to swap for the same time you own (e.g. 2nd week of July can be swapped for the first week in September.) Remember that *YOU CANNOT TRADE UP* to accomodations that are bigger than your own. Some member resorts are in such places as Hawaii, Puerto Rico and Colorado. Be sure to familiarize yourself with the rules and regulations governing this interchangeable ownership provision as well as all the covenants restricting your use of Interval or Time-shared properties.

CHAPTER 3

SINGLE FAMILY HOME

Depending on your taste and budget, large estates to modest homes are available throughout Florida. The least expensive home will be in the central areas of the state, the coastline areas will command higher prices and beachfront and riverfront properties are the most expensive. You can however, live close by the water at a reasonable price. Sometimes bargain can be found on beachfront or river front if the hone is older and requires some updating. I've seen some go for as low as $200,000.

On average, again depending on location, a 3 bed, 3 baths home starts in the $495,000 range and up.

By far the most economical way to go is to build a new home in a "planned community". Your broker will be able to direct you to desirable areas and communities. I suggest shopping for a building lot with a Broker - better buys can be had that way. Large development companies sell on a "Contract for Deed" base and the prices are considerably higher.

Once you have located a residential lot and arranged its purchase, shop around for a reliable builder. Builder's models will be available for you to choose from, but most builders will also build from your plans. After you have decided on a builder, do not be afraid to check some of his previous work. Ask for references and by all means go and talk to the owners of houses your builder has completed.

Ask how the irritating minor adjustment problems were handled by the builder, since these very often give a clear picture of the quality and integrity of the builder. Most new homes are covered with a warranty program to take care of major problems. If one is not offered, inquire about one.

If all the previous investigation was done during a short stay in Florida and you had to go back North to settle the arrangements for your move South, your home should be started and slated for completion to coincide with your arrival back into your chosen location. On the average, your builder needs 90 -120 days to complete your house. At this point, it may be a good idea to hire a building consultant that will keep an eye on the construction and will give you a bi-weekly or monthly progress reports. This will ensure that you are kept informed of the material actually used and the quality of the construction. Consultant fees will vary with the complexity of construction and your personal instructions, but they are well worth the money.

PRE-OWNED HOMES

For many of us, it isn't convenient or feasible to wait for the construction of a new home; therefore, purchasing a pre-owned home is the answer. Your real estate agent will be as knowledgeable about the house as the owner will divulge, and it is the duty of the agent to inform you of all problems real or suspected. Of course not all problems are readily visible and some owners may even hide some of the facts. However, there are a few things you can do while you are walking thru the house that will help you determine its condition.

When checking the plumbing, don't be afraid to look under the sinks by opening the cabinet doors. Check for leaks under the pipes and look at the condition of the couplings. Open the faucets while doing this so that if there is a leak you may see it. It will also show the amount of water pressure. Flush the toilets to see if the handle on the tank is working properly and how well it flushes. Check the shower heads, calcium deposit around the head indicates water hardness and the possibility of the same deposits inside the pipes which will eventually restrict water flow.

Check all sinks and tub drains (and while on the subject of water, later on don't forget to find out where the outside water spigots are located for convenient lawn care). Check the window encasements for water stains on inside walls which could mean leaks. Look up and check seams where walls and ceiling meets, for water stains which might indicate a leaky roof. If you notice cracks between ceiling and wall joints, and cracks at the corner joints of windows, it might indicate the house has not yet settled. Check the door knobs throughout and see if doors open, close, and lock easily. Make sure all windows have screens or that some will be provided. Check the condition of the water heater and its capacity and also the air conditioner's condition and capabilities {BTU's}.

Closet space is very important to some of us, so don't be afraid to check those also. Some sellers are very clever at hiding defects or even holes in the walls by placing furniture in front of these, so don't hesitate to peek behind. If the carpeting is badly soiled, request to have it professionally cleaned and ask for the receipt at closing. The same applies for the termite inspection (required by law) certificate. If the previous owners had pets, I would strongly suggest having a pest control company thoroughly spray the carpets for fleas BEFORE moving in.

The inside of the house is usually the area you are first introduced to and on which you might base your impressions, but you should inspect the outside of the house just as well. Check the outside walls for cracks that might let the rains or insects in too readily. Have the air conditioner turned on and listen to the compressor, a noisy, squeaky fan may indicate some servicing is needed. Check the soffits for "breathing areas" from the roof. Don't be swayed by the owner or realtor that emphasizes the "beautiful landscaping". The house is what you're buying, not the landscaping. If the house has a screened patio, check for tears in the screens and leaks along the inside walls.

If a pool is included, check for cracks; check the pump and filter and listen to it run. Find out when it was last serviced, and have the receipt for what services were rendered given to you at the closing also.

Naturally, you must allow for normal wear and tear when inspecting a house. But an unusual amount of repairs or disrepair can be reflected in the price you offer. When writing out the purchase contract, list all the items that you'd like included OR that you have been told would be included. Do not assume that the light fixtures, rods and drapes, appliances, some mirrors, etc. will be left there.

If you noticed certain pieces of furniture that would suit your lifestyle, approach the owners; sometimes they might be willing to negotiate separately for that sale. In these days of high energy cost, don't forget to look for the energy conscious house too.

Most homeowners feel that their house is worth more than it really is, so have your real estate agent do a comparative market~analysis for houses in the area that you are interested in. This will help you deal realistically with the owner and in turn your agent can confront the seller with the same realistic figures.

CHAPTER 4

MANUFACTURED HOMES

Perhaps the largest communities of mobile home parks are found in South Florida. They are so varied and numerous that I am only going to point out what to be on the look-out for and suggest an investigative trip or two before you either drive down with your new mobile home or have one delivered.

You can choose three basic types of parks or mobile home communities. One type that is becoming more common and increasingly popular among retirees is the park that leases the land space but at a guaranteed lifetime rent. This rental fee is fixed for the resident and thus make budgeting for fixed income people easier. Since the lot space is actually rented, there are no real estate taxes due and the rent usually covers all services that are provided.

A second kind of park is one in which the home owner actually purchases his own particular lot space and has a fee simple title to it. In this park the resident is responsible for all real estate taxes and other assessments on his lot just as if he owned a standard single family house. There are obvious tax advantages to this.

The third kind of mobile home park is one where the rental space is actually rented with no guarantee that the monthly fee will not escalate from time to time.

Mobile home park rules and regulations vary from one to another. Check them out carefully.

Many parks do not allow the following:
  Children
  Pets
  Double width
  Trucks, vans or motorcycles, RV or boat parking

Aside from the obvious rules and regulations, one should also inquire about the utilities provided in the park. The electrical service should be adequate for full air conditioning. Water pressure should be sufficient so that showers will not become trickles and fire protection through the hydrants will be sufficient. If recreational facilities are offered, find out if their care is included in the monthly fee or rent or if you will have other assessments.

More and more parks are becoming sophisticated communities and have their own "sales office" where you must purchase your mobile home. In others you will not be allowed to bring a mobile home in that is older than a set vintage.

If you think you might like to sell your mobile home in the future, check the rules on this since many park owners will not allow outside brokers. They will want to handle the sale themselves.

A mobile home is more affordable than a conventional house, and today come so well equipped and with attractive floor plans, upgrades and external looks, that many people prefer them to a standard home. ($75,000 will get you a gorgeous mobile home).

If you attach your mobile home, {today the preferred referral is "manufactured home") to a permanent foundation on a lot you own, you may be able to get up to a 95% mortgage for its purchase.

Some years past, Congress reclassified the mobile home as "manufactured housing". These "manufactured houses" sell anywhere from $35,000 to more than $100,000, depending on your tastes, space required and location of the park, while a conventional house usually starts at $120,000 and ranges upwards dramatically.

Mortgage Brokers and Mortgage Insurance Lenders tend to be more interested in the double-wide manufactured home (average price $60,000). Of course you will have to buy the lot which will be extra. Remember that you must have title to the lot before you can get a real estate mortgage for your manufactured home.

CHAPTER 5

RETIREMENT COMMUNITIES

Retirement communities have become prolific in Florida, being the ideal place to enjoy retirement while still full of life to enjoy all the amenities these places have to offer. Prices vary according to location, and amenities offered.

I could never list all, but to give you and idea I randomly picked two with different price ranges so that you can see the huge choices you have. First, from below $100,000's to upper $100,000's is HIGHLAND LAKES of Leesburg, in central Florida.

Located about 68 miles north of Orlando. Surrounded by 7 small lakes and natural wetlands, The Lakes allow model sailboats racing for the young at heart, catch-and-release fishing.

Numerous nature trails allow residents to observe wildlife such as foxes, eagles, cranes, herons and the other plentiful critters.

The large clubhouse is the focal point of many activities, including indoor walking track, heated indoor pool for the chilly winter months, indoor tennis, and pickleball courts are also available.   Outdoor options include lap pool, bocce ball courts, six tennis courts, etc.

Home size vary from 1040 square feet to 1852 square feet, offering 2 and 3 bedroom models, one or two car garage, screened lanai, open floor plans with family room. There are 938 build units at this time.

Easy access to the turnpike for the travelers to Orlando International airport, museums, malls, and of course all the Disney entertainment centers.

Most of the amenities listed above are pretty much standard in most retirement communities.

I happen to also live in central Florida in a huge retirement community, which at this time has approximately 150,000 inhabitants. The home prices starts in the upper 100's to over 1 million dollars, but does lack an indoor swimming pool.

So you can see the diversity is here. Google "55+ retirement communities" and you'll have hundreds of location to choose from.

CHAPTER 6

FINANCING

When you have made your choice to the type of home and location you want, star shopping around for the bank that will hold your mortgage should you need one. Most to the time the agents who sold you the property, or your real estate broker, will refer you to several banks in the area that are familiar with their developments. These financial institutions are valuable sources of information on the home you are about to buy.

The following is the information that will be required by the banks:

1. When considering your mortgage application, the loan officer is interested in the three "C's'" credit, character and capacity. They will want to know your job history, your credit references, outstanding debts, charge accounts, savings, life insurance policies, and most important of all, your income. What follows are the specifics your loan officer will require:

   a. The Social Security numbers of you, your spouse, your partners, or any other co-borrowers.

   b. Your previous address, if you have lived at your present one less than two years.

   c. The mailing address of your previous employer, if you have been employed less than two years at your currently listed place of employment. Not applicable if you are retired of course.

   d. Your gross monthly income, including that of your spouse and any other co-borrower.

You will need to supply your latest W-2 Tax Form. If you are self employed, you will need a financial statement, signed copies of your Federal Tax Return for the last two years, and if you have one, your edited profit and loss statement.

e. Your savings account number(s) with the name and address of your bank. All accounts will be checked by the lending institution.

f. A list of all liabilities and assets. If you own property, you will need the name and address of the lender if the property is mortgaged, the property's current value and the amount still due on any loan on the property.

g. The mortgagor will check your credit history. If you are aware of any past problems in your credit records, write an explanation and attach it along with the application.

h. You will also need a copy of the sales contract of your purchase. Many banks like to have their own appraiser take a look at the property you are buying.

i. Bring your checkbook along because you will have to pay for the appraisal and credit check up front unless the bank tells you otherwise.

One final note on arranging financing is very important: the Mortgage Contingency Clause. This is a statement that you should make a part of your purchase agreement whenever there is any doubt what-so-ever about your obtaining acceptable financing. Simply stated, this contingency clause protects you in the event that your mortgage request is denied and allows the return of your deposit. If this clause is not inserted in the purchase agreement and you cannot obtain your mortgage the seller may keep your deposit. When your mortgage is approved, have the bank notify the developer or seller of the property so the contingency can be removed from the contract. This will avoid any delay should work need to be done on your property prior to your taking possession because no work can be done while a contingency is in force.

CHAPTER 7

HOW TO FURNISH YOUR FLORIDA HOME

Most people move to Florida with the intention of starting out "NEW". But it isn't easy to leave the old life behind especially our old and reliable furniture.

What you should bring and what you should leave is an individual decision, but be aware of some differences in the Florida lifestyle as these will help you make up your mind about that "comfortable overstuffed chair".

Life in Florida is more casual than in most areas. It is outdoor oriented and as a result, homes are generally smaller but with large screened areas or patios. One thing you must remember is that Florida homes do not have basements and most do not have "attics" as you know them. Many have carports instead of garages, so you might find storage in Florida homes limited when compared to your home up North.

The Florida upholstered furniture pieces are usually done in foam rubber as it is more efficient in coping with the climate. But with air conditioning prevalent in most homes, any comfortable filler is fine.

Florida furniture is generally lighter and more "airy" in style than the heavier, darker northern pieces. This does not mean all your furniture has to be of the tropical ratan, wicker or bamboo. Many pieces, even antiques, do very well with the modern lines of Florida furniture. Coordination and compatibility is the key. Since your living areas may be smaller, both the size and amount of furniture must be reduced.

Light colors for rugs and walls will also do wonders in creating a feeling of space. A good idea is to make a trip to the News-Stand and pick up some magazines (Southern Living, Indian River Life, or have friend mail them too you) to catch up on the practical and fashionable trends of Florida living.

In conclusion, plan to dispose of the furnishings you're not really happy with. A "garage sale" or perhaps the new owners of your home may have use for some of your furnishings. Take advantage of this move to weed OUT THE OLD AND USELESS AND LOOK forward to creating a new environment to fit your new lifestyle.

CHAPTER 8

FLORIDA TAXES

The Constitution of the State of Florida prohibits a state income tax. The major portion of the state's revenue comes from the sales tax (exempt on groceries, medicine and professional services).

Florida residents have no state inheritance tax unless they are subject to a Federal estate tax, in which case the state of Florida collects the amount allowed as a deduction from the Federal estate tax.

Real estate taxes (county, city and school) are based on 100% valuation of the appraised value of the property whether business or residential. Homeowners are allowed $5,000 homestead exemption which means that the first $5,000 of assessed value is tax free. Application for this exemption, as prescribed by the State Constitution, must be filed with the property appraiser on or before March 1st each year by bonafide residents.

To qualify, an owner must reside on the property on January 1st. Subsequent applications to the original one are mailed by the property appraiser's office, but it is the responsibility of the taxpayer to be sure the application for exemption is received by the property appraiser's office prior to March first.

Legal residents who have lived in Florida the previous five (5) consecutive years, may apply to the property appraiser for additional homestead exemptions up to a maximum of $25,000 by 1982 (at which time all legislated exemptions become fully implemented).

To become a legal resident of Florida your must:

1. (a) Either register to vote or
   (b) file a certificate of domicile AND
2. If you operate or own a motor vehicle, have a
   Florida's drivers license and tags.

Additional exemptions are available for widows, disabled individuals and disabled veterans. Further details can be obtained from the property appraiser's office. Sale taxes vary from county to county.

CHAPTER 9

ADMINISTRATION OF JUSTICE

On January 1, 1973, a revised version of Article V of the Florida Constitution (the basis of the Florida Judicial System) became effective. We now have two systems: a trial court system, consisting of the circuit and county courts; and the appellate court system, which includes the district courts of appeal and the supreme court, and upon occasion the circuit court.

No other courts may be established by the state, any political party, or by any municipality (except Dade County).

The legislature is given the power to divide the state into appellate court districts and judicial circuits following county lines. The supreme court has the power to adopt all rules and procedures used throughout Florida's court system. The chief justice of the Supreme Court is the chief administrative officer of the entire judicial system and is chosen by a majority vote from among the justices. A chief judge for each district court of appeal is chosen by a majority vote of the judges in the district. A chief judge in each circuit court system is chosen from among the circuit judges. Each chief judge has the administrative responsibility of his/her district.

The Supreme Court

The supreme court, located in Tallahassee, is composed of seven justices, and is required to hear the following appeals:

a) Final Judgments of trial courts imposing the death penalty,

b) The validation of bonds or certificates of indebtedness and review rate actions of statewide agencies or utilities (when provided by general law).

They may also review:

a) Orders of trial courts and decisions of district courts of appeal involving constitutional issues or statutes at the federal or state levels,

b) Any decision of a district court of appeals that passes upon a question certified to be of great public interest, or is in conflict with a previous decision of another appellate court   or of the supreme court itself. Five justices constitute a quorum and concurrence of at least four justices is required for a decision

The District Court of Appeal

The state is divided into five appellate districts of continuous counties with a court in each district. These courts, often called the "Courts of Last Resort," hear appeals that may be taken as a matter of right, appeals from final judgments or orders of trial courts not directly appealable to the supreme court or a circuit court. They also have the power of direct review of administrative action as prescribed by general law. A panel of three judges is required for each case with a concurrence of two required for a decision.

The Circuit Court

The circuit courts are Florida's trial courts of general jurisdiction and have exclusive jurisdiction in all actions of law not vested in county courts. There are 20 judicial circuits. At the present time there are nine. These courts hear all civil cases over $5,000, all criminal felonies, all juvenile matters except traffic cases, all probate, guardianship, and incompetency

The Juvenile Court

The juvenile court is a separate court which comes under the jurisdiction of the circuit court. The procedure is quite different from an adult court and occurs as follows.

Juvenile is arrested and parents and the Children & Youth service (CYS) worker are notified. A decision is made to detain or release juvenile to his/her parents.

A meeting is set up with juvenile and CYS worker to provide material for an "intake" report which is sent to the state attorney. Based on this report, a decision is reached by the state attorney to file or drop the charge. If filed, an arraignment hearing is set.

If the juvenile pleads guilty, a sentencing date is ordered with a pre-disposition report. If the juvenile pleads not guilty at the arraignment, a hearing date is set. A public defender is provided if needed. If a juvenile is adjudicated delinquent, then a predisposition report is requested and a sentencing date is set. The judge determines a punishment at the sentencing hearing, e.g., probation, restitution, incarceration.

In certain situations a juvenile may be tried as an adult: The juvenile may waive his rights and request a jury trial. The state attorney may (after evaluating the intake report) bring the matter to the grand jury and request them to order the juvenile tried as an adult. If a juvenile is 14 or older, the state attorney may request that the judge hold a hearing and certify the youth to be tried as an adult. If a juvenile is 16 or 17 years old with a record of two prior adjudications of delinquency, one of which must be a felony, a state attorney can file the case directly in the adult court system after evaluation of the intake report.

The County Courts

The county courts have original jurisdiction in all criminal misdemeanor cases not handled by the circuit court including violations of county or municipal ordinances, all traffic offenses, all landlord-tenant litigations, and all civil cases up to $5,000, except those within exclusive jurisdiction of the circuit court. This court is often called the "People's Court."

SPECIAL FEATURES SECTION

CHAPTER 10

LIVING ON BOARD

If you've always dreamed of retiring to an easy life on board your boat, a life of gentle swaying, sounds of fish "a-leaping" and inexpensive rent, read on. Many people have sold their home, bought a boat and headed South without any foreknowledge of where they would be able to dock and live. Don't make this mistake. You just can't anchor anywhere in a river or dock in any marina and call it home. Stringent city and county laws dictate where you may anchor and for how long. Many marinas do not have facilities for live-aboard tenants, nor do they want them. You could find yourself going miles out of the area you wanted to live in to find a marina.

Write or call the local city hall's zoning department for precise information.

The up-keep of your floating home is a daily chore you might not have had to endure in colder Northern water. The warm waters of South Florida stimulate the growth of algae and barnacles, especially on the wooden keels of older boats.

The hot sun and salt air combine for faster deterioration of paint and varnish; even teak is victimized! What you dreamed of as lazy days of gentle swaying relaxation could turn into daily grind of up-keep.

Also if you must live on a fixed income, you might find the marina fees higher than anticipated and the up-keep more expensive than originally planned thus making your dream a nightmare.

Florida live aboard marinas can become supportive communities. If you are still working you may need to find a place near your job location. You will need to do lots of research. If you are truly retirees and can live anywhere, your marina choices will be easier to find.

I suggest you check "www.living-aboard.com" on your computer and you will find a wealth of information.

CHAPTER 11

PETS

Some of us who move to Southern Florida do so upon our retirement. The kids are grown and on their own and many times we acquire dogs or cats for companionship. Your dogs and cats will have to adjust to their new climate as much as you. Heat rash, fleas and ticks will be triple what you encountered in the past.

Don't forget to check the rules and regulations should you chose condominium, mobile home park or marina living to see if pets are allowed. Many of these communities have a size limitation or just don't allow pets at all.)

The following chapter on "heart worm" may seem a little technical, but all dog lovers who have not been exposed to this prevalent "southern discomfort" might appreciate knowing the cycle of the disease and so be able to prevent its development in their pets.

Heart worms are transmitted by mosquitoes. When a mosquito draws blood from a heart worms infected dog, it will infect the next dog it bites. Ingested by the mosquito, the blood which contains microdilariae (microscopic worms) undergoes a transformation to become infective larvae in about 14 to 21 days. These infective larvae are really miniature adults, small enough to live in the mosquito's body. The whole cycle of infection repeats itself over and over each time a dog is bitten. You may take preventive measures as soon as you arrive in Florida by having a veterinarian check your pet and give it pills to prevent infection.

Don't put it off; a dog can be infected for over a year before the telltale signs, such as coughing, lack of appetite, restlessness shows. By then it may be too late.

As for the fleas, keep in mind that households "without pets" also can become infested with fleas. Fleas are everywhere and as you walk in your yard, you may bring them into the house where they drop into the rugs and furniture and have a merry time multiplying. If you have no pets, you are their first target. So, when moving into a new home or condo, don't hesitate to spray or fog the entire area even before you move in. Of all the products on the market, I have found that the "Holiday Fogger" has been the best in controlling fleas. The fog penetrates into the carpet where it will last 2-3 months and kill fleas as they hatch in the fibers. But, there are other ways to fight back if you have a green thumb and like to engage in a little horticultural warfare.

Fleas reportedly flee from "Gliridia sepium", among other plants. It's a tropical American tree common in the West Indies, and it's found growing on some older homesteads in South Florida. Pioneer families used to strew leaves from the tree around the house to repel fleas.

Several shrubs, for your yard, popularly known as "fleabane" are also believed to repel fleas. Also, pesky fleas do not like the smell of some aromatic plants that humans find pleasant. For instance, you can boil a large quantity of pennyroyal, mint or sassafras in water, let the water cool and wash down your dog with the liquid. Your local nursery should be able to provide you with the plants and shrubs you seek.

NOTE: Here are a few other herbs that repel a variety of insects that you might want in your garden.

> BASIL near tomatoes repels worms and flies.
> MINT, SAGE, DILL AND THYME protect cabbage, cauliflower, broccoli and brussel sprouts from the cabbage moths. ONIONS and GARLIC protect your plants from Japanese beetles, carrot flies and aphids on lettuce and beans.

And, while in the garden, should ants become a problem pouring BOILING water on their hills will get rid of them.

CHAPTER 12

SCHOOLS

Last, but not least, in our special feature chapter is the school situation in Florida. Because of the monumental growth of Florida in the past few years, the counties find themselves floundering a little bit in the education department. After all, wasn't Florida supposed to be for Retired folks? So, how many retirees would need elementary schools for their families?

The average age of Florida today is getting younger, and young families need schools. The Education Department has risen to the challenge and new schools are sprouting up everywhere.

ATTENDANCE - A child is eligible for kindergarten if 5 years old on or before November lst of the 2017-2018 school year. October 1st of the 2017-2018 school year, and September 1st of the 2017-2018 school year, at which time September 1st will remain as the official entry date for 5 year olds. Successful kindergarten attendance is mandatory in most Counties. Contact the director of educational services for more information.

All children must be enrolled in a school program between the ages of 7 and 16 years. Students can legally withdraw from school at age l6. According to state law, parents are responsible for their child's school attendance.

ENROLLMENT - To enroll a student, contact the superintendent's office to determine which school your child should attend. The next step is to contact the principal at the designated school and he/she will outline the specific enrollment procedure and materials which you must provide prior to your child's entry into the system.

An immunization record is required as well as a certificate of health which is obtainable from physicians or from the Health Department. A birth certificate is also required.

If you are new to Florida you must be able to prove that you intend to become a resident. You may do this by obtaining auto license tags, voter registration, or by completing a "Declaration of Domicile," a form which states your intent to become a resident. These forms are available at the county clerk's office in the courthouse.

SCHOOL SESSION - The school year usually begins in the latter part of August. The school year runs for 210 days for elementary students. If your child is doing well in all subject areas and passes all the minimum competencies, he/ she will be exempted for the final 30 days of the school year. The school term for junior high and senior high students is 180 days. The summer session is 30 days and lasts for 4 hours/day.

SCHOOL RECORDS - All parents have the right to inspect all educational records of their child who is under 18 years of age. Pupils who have passed their 18th birthday have the right to inspect their own records. Each year parents are notified of the Family Rights and Privacy Act which governs access to and release of educational records.

CORPORAL PUNISHMENT - Under Florida Statutes, a teacher may administer corporal punishment to a pupil with general permission of the principal and in the presence of another adult who has been informed of the reason for the punishment. The parents do not have to be notified, but upon request, the administrator of the punishment must provide the parent with a written explanation of the reason for the punishment and the name of the other adult who was present.

So, if you do have school age children, get in touch with the school board in the area your child will attend and get as much information as possible. Try to get as much done prior to coming down.

Don't forget to inquire about school transportation. Public transportation in Florida, except for some in the larger cities, is practically nil. Your child may be able to ride the school bus provided by the county, or he may have to walk or ride his bike or be driven to school by you.

CHAPTER 13

HURRICANES

June 1st through October 31st is hurricane season in Florida. Many new comers to Florida have never been through a hurricane and tend to take a lackadaisical attitude when warned of an impending hurricane. Local Civil Defense officials report that this attitude is one of the greatest dangers of all.

Hurricanes should be respected but not feared. However, people should remember to be prepared and to plan ahead. Too many wait until the crisis occurs to try to do somethings dangerous.

The following are suggestions to help you should a hurricane warning occur in your locality: Know if you will have to leave your home and where you will go. Start stocking up on canned goods, batteries, candles and other storable items. Buy lumber and hardware you will need to prepare your house for a storm. Know what you will be doing with your boat and pets. Evaluate your landscape and trim your trees before a storm forms. **Never, never** wait until the last minute to make preparations. The purchase of necessary safety items can be accomplished anytime during the off-hurricane season and should always be on hand. The following is an example of the items you should always have ready for an emergency:

A portable radio with extra batteries
A lantern with fuel, or other type of lighting
Emergency cooking facilities, (sterno stove, canned heats, BBQ grill (for outdoor use only)
Canned goods, canned or dry milk, fruits, juices, soups, and a manual can opener
Dog and cat food

Bleach for purifying water if needed
Strong boards for boarding your windows

To board up your house, local lumber yards suggest using regular exterior sheathing grade plywood 1 inch thick. The lumber yard said use nails, but the Civil Defense suggested drilling holes and using a molly and wingnut. The boards can then be put on with ease and the wingnuts left for the next season.

You should have a seven day supply of non-perishable food that doesn't need to be heated. Buy batteries that will last for several hours as you may need to use your radio or flashlight for several continuous hours. Don't forget to gas up your car. Should the electricity fail after the storm, you won't be able to get gas for awhile.

Make plans to move your boat. According to the Coast Guard, it is best to take small boats out of the water and lash them down. A large boat should seek a sheltered area. Don't leave it in a marina; the personnel will not take care of it for you. Also, the bridges will be locked down as soon as they start to evacuate the barrier islands. If you have a large boat with a high mast, you may not be able to go under any bridges. Plan ahead.

Another thing to keep in mind is not to stock your freezer full. Should the electricity fail for several days, you could have hundreds of dollars in food losses and the very unpleasant task of cleaning a very smelly appliance. To protect what you do have in your freezer when a hurricane warning is given, put it on the coldest setting and open the door as seldom as possible. Listen for bulletins and local advisories. If the storm decides not to come your way, put away your supplies for the next time around.

If the hurricane *watch* is advanced to hurricane *warning*, this means the storm is expected within the next 24 hours.

If you live on a barrier island, in a mobile home park or in a flood plain, you may be asked to evacuate. Don't hesitate to heed the warning. Make sure you have prepared your home by bringing in all loose objects, boarding it up and, if in a mobile home, you have checked your tie-downs.

Turn your refrigerator and freezers to their coldest settings. Fill all available containers with water. This includes the tub and washing machine. If you have a pool, local pool builders suggest you pump your pool down about one foot only. DO NOT DRAIN it. Add at least three gallons of chlorine for each 5,000 gallons of water. Make sure you remove everything from your patio and turn off the electrical power to the pool.

If you have an attic ventilator (or wind turbines, which I neglected to remove in 2004 and lost my roof because of that) take it down and cap the hole, the strong winds will probably tear it off. If invited to a "hurricane party", don't drink too much as you will need your wits about you if you need to react quickly. During the hurricane, STAY INDOORS, even if the eye passes overhead. (The eye may last from several minutes to an hour or more.) Keep a window open on the side of the house opposite the wind. This will release built up air pressure and prevent your windows from exploding inward.

If you must or decide to evacuate your home, the Red Cross lists three alternatives to staying home. _One_, relocate outside the storm area. _Two_, stay with friends or relatives in the local area. _Three_, a last resort is to go to a Red Cross shelter.

Before you leave your home, turn off the main power switch to the electricity and listen to local media for the roads you should be leaving on. If leaving the area or going to friends, leave a day ahead. If you have to go to a shelter (these should be reserved for people with nowhere else to go) you must be able to fend for yourself. Do not expect hotel treatment. Bring sleeping bags, air mattresses or anything else to sleep on, medication, extra clothes, radios, flashlights, books, cards, a thermos of coffee and food to last for at least two days.

NEITHER SMOKING OR DRINKING is allowed in the shelters. _DO NOT BRING PETS_, they won't be allowed in the front door. Most Humane Societies do not have facilities to house animals during a hurricane. You need to plan ahead for the care of your pets. Try to take your pets with you out of the area or leave it with a friend, especially if the animal is old and unhealthy. If this isn't feasible and you must leave your pet at home, think of its safety. Bring your pet inside the house and provide enough food and water for the time you will be gone. Provide something high such as a table for the animal to jump on. Do not chain or tie up your pet; it must be able to swim or jump if necessary, and DO NOT tranquilize your pet.

Hurricanes are a very real danger and should be treated as such. To use an old quote, "An ounce of prevention is worth a pound of cure."

CHAPTER 14

ODDS AND ENDS

The following items were prompted by my own experience of my early years in Florida. Not being familiar with MILDEW, I wasn't aware that certain precautions should be taken. Several suitcases later, someone provided me with the following solution.

If you store your suitcases in an un-air conditioned garage, chances are that when it comes time to take a trip you may find your suitcases have acquired a "musty" odor, something less than pleasant to pack your clothes in. The culprit will probably be mildew.

To get rid of its odor, mix one cup of water with one cup of rubbing alcohol. Dip a cloth in the solution, wring it out, and wipe the inside of the suitcase. Then dry the interior of the suitcase in a good breeze. If the odor persists, wash the interior with thick suds made from mild soap, saddle soap or soap containing a germicide or fungicide. Then wipe with a damp cloth and dry it in an airy place. You can then prevent further mildew in your suitcase if you put a small bar of soap inside before you store it away.

The following information is in case you go on vacation and forget to clean out the refrigerator and food spoils or the electricity fails for a number of days during a hurricane and you are left with a very smelly appliance to clean. Here is what to do:

After you have disposed of the spoiled food, your first step is to check the drip pan underneath the refrigerator! freezer. Clean it out then wash the drip pan and the inside of your refrigerator/freezer with a solution of baking soda and water. Then go buy activated charcoal at an aquarium supply store and place a tray of the charcoal inside the refrigerator/ freezer. The charcoal will absorb the odor, but you may have to change the charcoal a couple of times before the smell is completely gone. Let's hope it won't happen to you.

Next I want to share with you the recipe for mango wine.
Mangoes are delicious in various ways, you can even freeze them and later serve them on ice cream or on your favorite cereals, but mango wine is the real treat. For 5 gallons of wine you will need the following:

    18 pounds of mangoes
    10 pounds of sugar
    l-1/4 teaspoon of grape tannin
    1 1/4 teaspoons of pectic enzyme
    5 tablespoons of fruit acid (lemon or lime juice)
    1 package champagne yeast
    5 teaspoons of liquid bisulphite

Peel and pit the mangoes and mash them. (Don't put them in a blender, just squash them). Add the sodium bisulphite mix thoroughly and allow the mixture to sit for 24 hours. Add all the other ingredients, mix thoroughly and leave the mixture in an open pot or pail for three days. Stir at least once a day. Strain the mixture and put the liquid into a 5 gallon water bottle or some container that has a lock. It will be ready to drink in two weeks, or it will keep indefinitely as long a the seal isn't broken.

Once opened, the wine should be refrigerated,(if you want you can substitute the 10 pounds of sugar with a one gallon of honey.)

If you have a fireplace and you cut down a mango tree and decide to burn it either as an open fire, or in your fireplace DON'T DO IT. People break out in a rash by just coming in contact with the sap of the mango tree. If you burn the wood, the same sap creates a smoke that is very irritating to the eyes. When the Palmetto Expressway was built, some old mango groves were bulldozed and burned and people for miles around complained of itching eyes. The mango, poison ivy, poisonwood tree and the brazilian pepper tree (or Florida Holly) are all members of the ANACARDIACEAE family. None of them should be used as firewood.

CHAPTER 15

SOLAR ENERGY

If you are energy conscious, as most of us should, there is no better place to use solar energy than Florida. With rebates and tax credits in place, it will make your system affordable. With 360 days of sunshine, how can you go wrong. It is a cost effective way to generate hot water for your entire house, and can be used in any climate.

If you have a large home starting with a solar hot water system is ideal. One solar panel fits on the roof, facing south west, a pump circulate the water through tubes inside the panel to a glass lined storage tanks that is part of the installation system. Be careful, the water gets hot, but its care free.

If you have a pool, solar panels will make the water confortable, and with a back up heater, gas or electric for winter, you can use your pool year around. I highly recommend Heliocol panels as they are made of tubing which will allow the wind to flow thru in a storm. I've seen more flat water envelope type panels sail off into the wind when it flew under them.

Next is the photovoltaic panels (electric) which can help alleviate the electrical cost of your home. With these you are partially off the grid during daylight hours. At night, it reverts back to your current electric provider. You can be completely off the grid by installing an array of lithium batteries to have night time use of the stored electricity. Again rebates and tax credit will alleviate your cost. There is nothing more worthwhile seeing than the look on a home owner's face when he watches his electric meter flow backwards to the communnity source.

Make sure you get a reputable company to install your system. Check out their references. Today, there are too many con artists in the aisles, waiting for you to jump at the cheap prices they may offer for their services.

FLORIDA TRIVIA

The state of Florida has had many nicknames, including the Alligator State, Everglade State, Orange Blossom State, and Peninsula State. The official nickname of Florida is now the Sunshine State. The state motto is "In God we trust", the state song is "Swannee River" (Old folks at Home) by Stephen Foster, the state bird is the mockingbird, the state Flower is the fragrant and lovely orange blossom, and the state tree is the Sabal Palmetto.

Florida entered the union on March 3, 1845, as the 27th state and its capital is Tallahassee. Florida's mild climate and sub-tropical beauty make it one of the first places many people consider when thinking of a vacation or a retirement home. An average of 60% of winter days have sunshine.

Annual rainfall averages 52.8 inches, but there is a variation from year to year. In southern Florida crops are grown in the fall, winter and spring. From June through November the state is liable to hurricanes, especially along the keys and the lower end of the peninsula. Sand, of course, is the common ingredient of most of Florida's soil.

Exclusive of cultivated plants, more than 3,000 flowering species grow in Florida. Among the wild flowers are the blue lupines, mimosa, blue iris, white calla, and clematis. Some beautiful wild vines include the Cherokee rose, Carolina yellow jasmine and trumpet vine.

Some other popular exotic plants include the golden begonia and the bougainvillea, whose brilliant coloring decorate the landscaping in many southern Florida homes. Other well known blossoms are the poinsiatta, the gardenia, the camelia, hibiscus, oleander and azalea.

Many of Florida's native animals, such as the black bear, deer, wildcat, Florida panther also known as montain lion, mink, and otter have become scarce.

The alligator as been removed from the endangered species list, and you see them in retention ponds, and on the golf courses. DO NOT APPROACH THEM. Turtles, frogs, lizards, rabbits, squirrels, raccoons, and opossums are still numerous. But the most enjoyable and picturesque are the water birds such as the gulls, herons, pelicans and their relatives.

If you're a beach goer, you'll see most of these birds on or near the beaches. Florida's beaches are world famous and we have more of them than any place. Miles and miles of white sand border the clear blue-green waters with temperatures that invite participating in all water sports and recreation.

After the beaches, sports and fishing, there are many other attractions in Florida, from the serene natural beauty of the everglades to the magnificent array of Disney World. In South and Central Florida there are three art centers you may be interested in. They are the Ringling Art Museum in Sarasota, the Norton Art Gallery in West Palm Beach, and the Research Studios in Maitland. Marine Studios, the "Oceanarium", about 30 miles South of St. Augustine on Matanzas Inlet, has 20,000 species of salt water fish. There are similar Oceanariums in Miami and Daytona Beach. Let's not forget Cape Canaveral on the central east coast - NASA satellite launchings has delighted many of us.

For the musically inclined, a musical event of note is the "Bach Festival" given annually at Winter Park.

Another source of recreation is the many fresh water springs where you may picnic, swim or see the water life from glass-bottomed boats. Such springs are Sakulla Springs, south of Tallahassee and Silver Springs near Ocala; then you have Cypress Gardens on Lake Eloise; you also have the Garden of Resurrection on Mountain Lake Sanctuary in Lake Wales on Route 60, where the "Singing Tower" erected by Edward Bok is located (one of the most famous places in Florida). There are also many state parks to choose from with Florida Caverns (covering 1,187 acres) near Marianna, probably the most famous.

The one thing I'd like to mentioned is that Florida is known as the "LIGHTNING CAPITAL OF THE WORLD." Don't take chances in a thunder storm. My husband poopooed the idea only once. Him and his friend were on the golf course, a storm was brewing, but they figured they had another hour before the rain would start. They both woke up in the hospital. My husband was safe, except for his bruised ego, but his friend had been closer to the palm tree that the lightning hit, was thrown back hard and broke his arm. If you can hear thunder you are close enough to be hit by lightning. Fact is that lightning can hit as far as 100 miles from the thunder storm head.

Wherever you choose, you'll find Florida truly a place with a relaxed lifestyle which will soon ease the shattered nerves and stressful pressure so common to city living.

SUMMARY

For whatever reason you decide to purchase real estate in Florida, this handbook is intended to guide you and give you ideas of what to look out for and suggestions to save you time and possibly money.

My observations deals with central and South Florida, my place of residence and also since this is the most popular and fastest growing parts of the state.

The information presented was based on personal experience gathered from professional dealings. It is not to be construed as advice on where or what to buy. The information is just that - something on which to base your decision. The most important advice that I can give is that the prospective buyer should always consult an attorney, BUT not just any attorney, preferably one who is a local resident and knowledgeable in the area and *laws of the State of Florida.*

I hope you have enjoyed this handbook and that it has provided you with information you needed to make your move more pleasurable.

20 WAYS TO TELL YOU'RE GROWN UP:

1. Your houseplants are alive, and you can't smoke any of them.
2. Having sex in a twin bed is out of the question.
3. You keep more food than beer in the refrigerator.
4. 6:00 AM is when you get up, not when you go to bed.
5. You heard your favorite song in the elevator.
6. You watch the weather channel.
7. Your friends marry and divorce instead of "Hook up" and "Break up".
8. Jeans and a sweater no longer qualify as "dressed up".
9. You go from 130 days of vacation to 14.
10. You're the one calling the police because the #$%^* kids next door won't turn down the stereo.
11. Older relatives feel comfortable telling sex jokes around you.
12. You don't know what time Taco Bell closes anymore.
13. Your car insurance goes down and your payments go up.
14. You feed your dog Science Diet instead of McDonalds leftovers.
15. Sleeping on the couch makes your back hurt.
16. Dinner and a movie is the whole date instead of the beginning of one.
17. You go to the drug store for Ibuprofen and antacid, not for condoms and pregnancy tests.
18. A $4.00 bottle of wine is no longer "pretty good shit."
19. 90% of the time you spend in front of your computer is for real work.
20. You drink at home to save money bef ore going to a bar.
21. You read this entire list looking desperately for one sign that doesn't apply to you and can't find one. HAHAHA! Have a nice day.